# RABBITS

Published in Great Britain in 2018
by Wayland

Copyright © Hodder and Stoughton, 2017

Editor: Elizabeth Brent
Produced for Wayland by Dynamo
Written by Pat Jacobs

MIX
Paper from
responsible sources
FSC® C104740
FSC
www.fsc.org

ISBN: 978 1 5263 0144 4

10 9 8 7 6 5 4 3 2 1

Wayland, an imprint of
Hachette Children's Group
Part of Hodder and Stoughton
Carmelite House
50 Victoria Embankment
London EC4Y 0DZ

An Hachette UK Company
www.hachette.co.uk
www.hachettechildrens.co.uk

Printed and bound in China

**Picture acknowledgements:**

**iStock:** Eric Isselée; p2 tyler olson, UroshPetrovic, SurkovDimitri;
p3 Dorottya_Mathe; p4 GlobalP; p6 Eric Isselée, Julia Mashkova, matooker,
GlobalP; p7 Susan Schmitz, GlobalP, Eric Isselée; p8 chengyuzheng, 5second,
Dorottya_Mathe, Erik Lam; p9 suemack, indavostrovska, MGStockPhotography,
Craig Dingle; p10 chengyuzheng; p11 &#169 CJKPhoto; p12 Elgars Retigs;
p13 XiXinXing, gurinaleksandr; p14 &#169 Norman Chan, -slav-, Toshiro Shimada;
p15 SeashoreDesign, Stefano Tinti; p16 Bronwyn8, vydrin; p17 Silke Dietze,
baramee2554, GlobalP, kali9; p18 Marco Hegner, Nikolay Suslov; p19 Ramaboin,
coramueller; p20 Phillip Danze, photobac; p21 wzooff, Dmitry Ersler, gutaper;
p22 Elgars Retigs; p23 photosaint, lindavostrovska, bazilfoto, cynoclub;
p24 Murmakova, chengyuzheng; p25 GlobalP; p26 Milos Stojanovic, FtLaudGirl,
justtscott, William Attard McCarthy, Voren1, ALEXIUZ; p27 AnikaSalsera,
akiyoko, feedough, Marina Maslennikova; p28 Voren1, Eric Isselée;
p29 Stefan Petru Andronache; p32 CPaulussen;
Front cover : Eric Isselée; Back cover: iava777

**Shutterstock:** p5 tr Imageman; p10 c Stephen Rees;
p17 cl Goldfinch4ever; p24 Samuel Borges Photography

**Alamy:** p10 Janet Horton; p12 ableimages;
p25 Arco Images GmbH

Every attempt has been made to clear copyright.
Should there be any inadvertent omission, please
apply to the publisher for rectification.

The website addresses (URLs) included in this
book were valid at the time of going to press.
However, it is possible that contents or
addresses may have changed since the
publication of this book.
No responsibility for any such changes can be
accepted by either the author or the Publisher.

# CONTENTS

# YOUR RABBIT
## FROM HEAD TO TAIL

Rabbits make great pets and each one has its own personality – they can be as playful as puppies and as mischievous as kittens. Rabbits are sociable creatures and enjoy spending time with people, but they need a bunny buddy, too.

**Eyes:** Rabbits' eyes are high up on the sides of their head so they can see in every direction and spot predators approaching from behind and above.

**Tail:** Rabbits sometimes wag their tail when they are annoyed or don't want to do as you ask.

**Hind legs:** Rabbits' long, strong hind legs allow them to stand up tall to look for predators, and to run fast to escape them.

**Ears:** The shape of rabbits' ears allows them to hear sounds more than three kilometres away. They can also hear high-pitched sounds that humans can't.

**Whiskers:** A bunny's whiskers are the width of its body, so they warn the rabbit if it is about to enter a narrow tunnel where it could get stuck.

**Teeth:** Rabbits' teeth never stop growing, but they are worn down by grinding up tough plants.

**Nose:** Rabbits have a great sense of smell, as well as extra scent organs called Jacobson's organs in the roof of their mouth. This helps them to detect predators before they see them.

# RABBIT FACTS

- Rabbits can run at speeds of up to 30 miles (48 km) an hour.

- A heavyweight British rabbit called Darius is 1.32 metres long and weighs almost 25 kg.

**Paws:** The bottom of rabbits' feet are padded with fur to cushion them.

# BUNNY BREEDS

Rabbits range in size from the cute little Netherland Dwarf, which is about the size of a guinea pig, to giant breeds that grow as large as a medium-sized dog. Here are a few of the most popular breeds:

**Rex** rabbits have a thick, velvety coat that is lovely to stroke. They make good house rabbits and are said to have a cat-like personality.

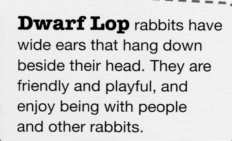

**Dwarf Lop** rabbits have wide ears that hang down beside their head. They are friendly and playful, and enjoy being with people and other rabbits.

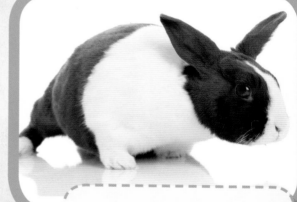

**Dutch** rabbits have a V-shaped white patch on their face and a white front. They are gentle, friendly and intelligent so they make great pets.

**English Spot** rabbits are medium-sized with a white coat and coloured markings. They are lively, inquisitive pets that need plenty of exercise.

**Harlequin** rabbits are gentle, curious pets that enjoy playing and like to be the centre of attention. They need lots of space and can live indoors or outside.

**Angora** rabbits are covered in long hair, which means they need grooming every day. For this reason, they are not the best choice for a busy family.

**Flemish Giant** rabbits are one of the largest breeds. They are good-natured and get on well with other pets, so they make great house rabbits.

**Belgian Hares** are rabbits, despite their name. They have a long, slim body and long legs and ears. They are one of the most energetic and intelligent breeds.

# CHOOSING YOUR RABBIT

In the wild, rabbits live in groups. They need company so it's best to get at least two, otherwise your bunny will be lonely. Before you buy or adopt a rabbit, check that its eyes are sparkling, its teeth meet up properly at the front and its ears are clean.

## BABY  ADULT?

Baby bunnies are adorable, but they can be destructive and it can be hard to tell if they are male or female. By choosing an adult, you can find out about your new pet's personality and, if you get one from a rescue centre, it will have been health-checked and neutered.

## LONG-  SHORT-HAIRED?

Long-haired rabbits are cute bundles of fur, but they are high-maintenance pets. While short-haired bunnies need grooming about once a week, long-haired rabbits must be brushed every day, or their fur will get matted and their skin may tear.

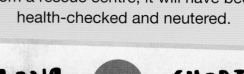

## LARGE or SMALL?

Giant bunnies make great pets, if you have space for them. They will need to live in the house or in a shed with a large run. Dwarf rabbits are easier to handle and live up to three times longer, but they still need lots of space to exercise.

## MALE or FEMALE?

Unneutered male rabbits spray urine and unneutered females can be very territorial, but both make good pets once they have been neutered. Rabbits can mate when they are just 10 weeks old, so if you get an unneutered pair, make sure they are the same sex.

## INDOOR or OUTDOOR RABBIT?

Rabbits make good house pets, if you bunny-proof your home. You'll be able to spend more time with them and they will probably get more exercise than they would in an outdoor run. Outdoor rabbits need a large, predator-proof cage and run.

# HOME SWEET HOME!

Your rabbit needs a clean, safe hutch to live in, where it can eat, sleep and rest – and hide if it feels scared. It also needs plenty of room to hop, run, jump and stretch out for a snooze. Here's how to create the perfect pad for your bunny:

Your rabbit needs room to stretch out, and to stand up on its back legs without touching the ceiling.

Line the sleeping area with newspaper and fresh hay.

A lock will keep your pets safe inside.

## PET CHECK ☑

Does your bunny have:

- enough room?
- a safe exercise run?
- its own food bowl?
- a water bowl or bottle?
- clean bedding?

## UNDERSTAND YOUR PET

Please put me in my run for a hop about in the early morning and late afternoon. That's when I am at my most active!

## KEEP IT CLEAN!

- Clean out the toilet area every day
- Clean out the hutch once a week
- Only use pet-safe cleaning products

Line the eating area with newspaper and wood shavings.

Put newspaper and woodshavings down to make a toilet area, away from the sleeping area.

Choose a hutch with a mesh door to let in fresh air.

Your rabbit will need a place to exercise – this can be an outdoor or indoor run, or a rabbit-proofed room in your home.

# MAKING FRIENDS

## INTRODUCING YOURSELF

The best way to get to know your new friend is by sitting quietly on the floor. Rabbits are naturally friendly and inquisitive so if you hold out a treat, such as a piece of carrot, your bunny will probably come to you.

Give your bunny a chance to get used to the sounds and smells of its new home before you try to play with it. Rabbits are quite timid – they need to know they have a safe place to hide if they get scared because they are prey to many animals.

Play gently alongside your new pet. Most rabbits prefer not to be picked up or held. Let them show you what they like.

## TAKE IT SLOWLY

Rabbits can't see very clearly and they have a blind spot in front of their nose. They may get frightened if you approach them suddenly, especially from behind, because this is what a predator would do.

## HOW TO STROKE YOUR BUNNY

Most rabbits like being stroked on the forehead and around the shoulders. They may not like being touched on the ears, feet, stomach or tail.

## UNDERSTAND YOUR PET

My favourite companion is another rabbit. Predators, like cats and dogs, are not my natural friends, and I may bully guinea pigs.

## OTHER PETS

Make sure your new rabbit is safe inside a cage before introducing other pets, and don't leave them alone together unless you know they will not hurt each other.

# RABBIT RATIONS

A rabbit's main food should be good-quality hay. Chewing on hay wears its teeth down so they don't grow too long.

## SPECIAL TREATS

Rabbits love fresh vegetables, but if they have too many they won't eat their hay (which keeps them healthy) and they may get diarrhoea. Leafy vegetables, carrots and broccoli make good bunny treats, but they should never have peas, beans, corn, rhubarb leaves, potatoes, onions or garlic.

## STRANGE, BUT TRUE

Because wild rabbits have to survive on poor-quality grass, they eat some of their droppings to get as much goodness from their food as possible. These special soft droppings are usually produced at night. You may see your rabbit sucking them directly from its bottom.

## WATER

A rabbit needs as much water as a medium-sized dog. A water bottle with a metal spout is better than a bowl of water, which can get dirty or be knocked over.

## WEIGHT WATCHING

Pet rabbits are not as active as those in the wild, so if they eat too many treats they can easily put on weight. An overweight rabbit can't groom itself properly and will suffer from lots of health problems.

## DAILY DIET ✓

Each day, your rabbit should have:

- a bundle of hay the size of its body
- a handful of fresh greens
- a tablespoon of green rabbit pellets

When you stroke your bunny, you should be able to feel its spine and ribs.

# DAY-TO-DAY CARE

Checking on your rabbit every day is the most important part of being a good pet owner. You should make sure its droppings look normal, that it is eating and drinking and that it doesn't seem unwell, or in pain.

Your vet can trim your rabbit's teeth and claws if they get too long.

## GROOMING

Rabbits groom themselves and their friends, but if they swallow a lot of hair it can get stuck in their stomach and cause a serious problem. That's why it's important to brush a short-haired bunny every week and a long-haired rabbit every day.

## TEETH AND CLAWS

Keep an eye on your rabbit's teeth and claws to make sure they're not getting overgrown. If its teeth get too long, your bunny won't be able to eat. Pet rabbits may not wear their claws down enough, especially if they live indoors, and overgrown claws can get ripped out.

## UNDERSTAND YOUR PET

Please be gentle when you brush my coat because I've got very delicate skin.

## PESKY PARASITES

Rabbits may pick up fleas and ticks, so check for signs of these when you're grooming your bunny. Look inside the ears, too, in case your pet has ear mites.

Visit the vet if your bunny's shaking its head and scratching its ears. It might be suffering from ear mites.

## BATH BAN

Rabbits hate getting wet and shouldn't be given a bath because they will panic and may injure themselves. If your bunny gets dirty, it's best to spot-clean the area with a little water and some pet shampoo.

## FLY STRIKE

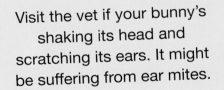

If rabbits have dirty fur, perhaps because they have diarrhoea or are too old or overweight to clean themselves properly, flies may lay their eggs there and maggots could burrow into their skin, so check your rabbit every day in summer, especially around its bottom.

# HEALTH AND SAFETY

Rabbits may be attacked by dogs, cats, foxes, stoats, weasels, badgers and birds of prey, so make sure their cages and runs are secure. Rabbits thump the ground with their back legs if they sense a predator nearby, so if you hear that sound, check that your pet is safe.

## INDOOR HAZARDS

From your bunny's point of view, an electric cable is just waiting to be chewed – and an electric shock could kill it. Rabbit-proof your home by lifting any cables out of reach or covering them with strong plastic tubing.

It's best to play with your bunny at ground level and let an adult pick it up if necessary, because rabbits can break their spine if they fall.

## NEUTERING

Getting your rabbits neutered makes them more friendly, better-behaved pets and saves them from a lot of health problems. Because rabbits have so many predators in the wild, they have lots of kittens. An unneutered female rabbit can have more than 70 kittens in just one year.

# VACCINATIONS

Your pet can catch deadly diseases, including myxomatosis and viral haemorrhagic disease, from wild rabbits and insects. There are no cures for these, so it's important to have your bunny vaccinated against them.

## UNDERSTAND YOUR PET

Please remember I'm wearing a fur coat, so keep my cage in the shade in summer and don't leave me in a hot room.

# POISONOUS PLANTS

Common plants that are poisonous for rabbits include bindweed, buttercups, elder, foxgloves, ivy, lupins, laburnum, oak leaves, privet and rhubarb, as well as apple seeds and many types of wood. Search online for a full list.

# BUNNY BEHAVIOUR

In the wild, rabbits explore the world around them by sniffing, nudging, chewing and digging. They can be mischievous and don't give up easily.

## CHEWING AND DIGGING

Chewing and digging are part of a rabbit's natural behaviour, so you can't blame them for trying to chew through the table leg or dig up the floor. It's best to give them toys they can chew and a sandpit or box full of shredded paper so they can behave naturally without causing damage.

## SCENT-MARKING

Rabbits have scent glands under their chins so you might see your bunny rubbing its chin against everything that it considers to be part of its territory – which could include you.

## BUNNY BINKIES

If your rabbit jumps in the air like a jack-in-the-box, twists its body and flicks its head and feet, it's performing a 'binky'. This means you have a very happy bunny.

## BORED BUNNY

If a rabbit starts grooming itself more often than usual it could be a sign of boredom, especially if it lives alone. A bored rabbit may also chew its cage and throw its toys or food bowl around.

## NOSE TWITCHING

Rabbits are well-known for twitching their noses and it's a sign of how interested they are in what's going on. If there's a lot of activity nearby, their nose may twitch at great speed. When it's quieter and they are relaxed, this will slow down or stop.

## UNDERSTAND YOUR PET

I have an extra, clear eyelid. Sometimes when I'm asleep I close it and I look like I'm sleeping with my eyes open.

# COMMUNICATION

Rabbits make their feelings known through their body position, ears, tail and the noises they make. Here's a guide to what your bunny is trying to tell you:

## BUNNY BODY LANGUAGE

When a rabbit is happy and relaxed it will flop down on to its side or roll on to its back with its eyes closed. If your bunny's feeling friendly, it will face you and may even give you a nudge, but if you've done something to upset it, it will turn its back. You can try doing the same if your rabbit does something you don't like.

## BUNNY CHAT

Some rabbits have a lot to say, while others are fairly quiet. Here are some examples of bunny noises and what they mean:

- **Soft tooth grinding:** I'm happy.
- **Chattering teeth or loud tooth grinding:** I'm in pain.
- **Muttering:** I'm angry or unhappy.
- **Growling or hissing:** I'm very angry.
- **Squealing:** I'm in pain or very frightened.
- **Clucking:** I'm relaxed.

## UNDERSTAND YOUR PET

If I suddenly become aggressive or start hiding, I may be ill or in pain.

## BEWARE!

An angry rabbit will growl or grunt and may flick its tail from side to side. This could be a warning that it's getting ready to bite, so it's best to back off.

## EXPRESSIVE EARS

The position of a rabbit's ears is a clue to how it's feeling.

- **Flicking ears:** I want to play.

- **Ears up and turned forwards:** I'm happy.

- **Ears turning sideways, then backwards:** I'm getting annoyed.

- **Ears tilted forwards:** I'm curious.

- **Ears tilted far back:** I'm cross so leave me alone.

- **Ears lowered and facing downwards:** I'm very unhappy and might be ill.

# TRAINING

Training your rabbit is fun for you both. Always use treats to reward your bunny when it does as you ask. Never punish it for doing the wrong thing because your rabbit will become scared of you. Clicker training is a good way to start.

## CLICKER TRAINING

Dog-training clickers might be too loud for a rabbit, so try using a retractable ballpoint pen. Click the pen, wait for a second, then give your bunny a treat. Move farther away and click again, then give your rabbit the treat if it comes to you. Repeat this several times.

## HERE, BUNNY!

Once your rabbit comes to you when it hears the clicker, start calling its name after each click before handing over the treat. Repeat this several times, then try calling without the clicker to see if your rabbit comes to you when it hears its name.

## HOME TIME

Training your rabbit to go back into its cage or carrier will save you from having to catch it. Sit close to the cage and use the clicker to call your pet, then put a treat inside. Repeat this several times while calling, 'Home!' Then try this without the clicker.

## LITTER TRAINING

Put a layer of newspaper in a shallow tray and cover it with hay, or litter suitable for rabbits (not cat litter). Scoop up a few droppings and scatter them in the tray to encourage your bunny to use it.

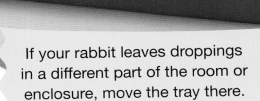

If your rabbit leaves droppings in a different part of the room or enclosure, move the tray there.

## TRAINING TIPS

• Only have one animal in the room during training.

• There should be no noise except the clicker and your voice.

• Training should only last a few minutes.

• Make sure your bunny has mastered one trick before moving on to the next.

• If your rabbit isn't interested, stop and try again later.

## UNDERSTAND YOUR PET

I'm cleverer than you think. I can learn to jump through a hoop and roll a ball, too.

# FUN AND GAMES

Rabbits are very active animals and need at least three hours of exercise every day. They love to play, so try some of these games and activities to see which your bunny likes best.

Stuff a kitchen roll tube with hay and hide a treat inside for your bunny to find.

## THROWING TOYS

Rabbits like toys they can hold in their mouths and throw about, but don't expect them to play 'fetch'. You will be the one who has to bring them back.

## TOPPLING TOYS

Most rabbits enjoy knocking things over, so set up some skittles, plastic bottles or a pyramid of balls or plastic bricks, then let your bunny loose.

Remove any parcel tape and staples from boxes.

## MAKE A RABBIT PLAY AREA

Create a cardboard city using boxes, tubes and tunnels and include a box full of shredded paper for burrowing. Cut windows and doors in the large boxes and add some toys, such as balls with bells inside, for extra bunny fun.

## WHEN TO PLAY

Rabbits are most active in the early morning and early evening, so this is the best time to play with them. When your bunny gets to know you, it will come and tell you that it wants to play by circling round your feet or pulling at your clothes.

# RABBIT QUIZ

How much do you know about your rabbit pal? Take this quiz to find out.

**1** **Which of these rabbits is the size of a medium dog?**

   a.  English Spot
   b.  Belgian Hare
   c.  Flemish Giant

**4** **Why do rabbits rub their chins against things?**

   a.  To scent-mark them
   b.  To scratch their chins
   c.  Because they are bored

**2** **Which of these rabbits has long hair?**

   a.  Angora
   b.  Harlequin
   c.  Rex

**5** **How often should you groom a short-haired rabbit?**

   a.  Every day
   b.  Every week
   c.  Every month

**3** **How often should you clean out your rabbit's hutch?**

   a.  Every day
   b.  Every week
   c.  Every month

**6** Which of these vegetables is not suitable for rabbits?

    a. Carrots
    b. Broccoli
    c. Onions

**10** How is a rabbit feeling if its ears are tilted forwards?

    a. Happy
    b. Curious
    c. Angry

**7** Which of these plants is bad for rabbits?

    a. Buttercups
    b. Grass
    c. Dandelions

**8** What is a 'binky'?

    a. A baby bunny
    b. A rabbit toy
    c. A 'happy bunny' jump

**9** When are rabbits most active?

    a. At night
    b. Early morning and late afternoon
    c. At lunchtime

# QUIZ ANSWERS

**1** Which of these rabbits is the size of a medium dog?

c. Flemish Giant

**2** Which of these rabbits has long hair?

a. Angora

**3** How often should you clean out your rabbit's hutch?

b. Every week

**4** Why do rabbits rub their chins against things?

a. To scent-mark them

**5** How often should you groom a short-haired rabbit?

b. Every week

**6** Which of these vegetables is not suitable for rabbits?

c. Onions

**7** Which of these plants is bad for rabbits?

a. Buttercups

**8** What is a 'binky'?

c. A 'happy bunny' jump

**9** When are rabbits most active?

b. Early morning and late afternoon

**10** How is a rabbit feeling if its ears are tilted forwards?

b. Curious

# GLOSSARY

**breed** – Named rabbit breeds have special features, such as a particular body shape or fur pattern, and all members of a breed will look more or less the same.

**clicker** – A useful tool that makes a sound that is only heard during training, and is always the same.

**diarrhoea** – Droppings that are much more liquid than normal.

**fleas** – Blood-sucking insects that cause itching and may carry diseases.

**grooming** – Keeping a rabbit's coat in good condition.

**hay** – Hay is dried grass. Any good-quality grass hay is suitable for rabbits, but avoid alfalfa because it is too fattening.

**instinct** – Natural behaviour that is automatic, not learned, such as a rabbit's instinct to dig and chew things.

**Jacobson's organs** – Two tube-like organs in the roof of the mouth that recognise chemicals in smells such as urine, as well as chemical signals given by other animals.

**kitten** – A baby rabbit.

**mating** – When a male and female animal get together to breed. Rabbits are well-known for being ready to mate at a young age and having large numbers of kittens.

**matted (fur)** – If long-haired rabbits aren't brushed every day, their fur can quickly get so tangled that it forms mats. These can pull on a rabbit's skin and may even tear it.

**mites** – Tiny creatures that are related to spiders.

**myxomatosis** – A deadly rabbit disease, which is spread by biting insects, such as fleas. It causes puffy swellings around a rabbit's face.

**neutering** – An operation that stops rabbits having kittens. Neutered rabbits make better, healthier pets, so it is recommended for both males and females.

**parasite** – An animal that lives in or on another creature and feeds from it (often by sucking its blood).

**predator** – An animal that hunts and eats other creatures.

**prey** – An animal that is hunted and killed by others.

**scent-marking** – In the wild, scent is important to rabbits because they live underground in dark burrows. They use scent glands under their chin to mark their territory and members of their colony.

**territorial behaviour** – Rabbits that have not been neutered mark their territory by spraying urine and leaving smelly droppings around the area. Neutering usually stops this behaviour.

**tick** – A small, round parasite that feeds on blood. Ticks look like warts or blood blisters when they are feeding.

**vaccination** – Injections that protect rabbits from serious diseases, such as myxomatosis and viral haemorrhagic disease.

**viral haemorrhagic disease** – This disease spreads very easily and kills rabbits in just a few days. Fortunately, pets can be vaccinated against this deadly illness.

# INDEX

TH 20(4(18